USDA

United States
Department of
Agriculture

Forest Service

Pacific Northwest
Research Station

General Technical
Report
PNW-GTR-798
July 2009

Interagency Strategy for the Pacific Northwest Natural Areas Network

Todd M. Wilson, Reid Schuller, Russ Holmes, Curt Pavola, Robert A. Fimbel, Cynthia N. McCain, John G. Gamon, Pene Speaks, Joan I. Seevers, Thomas E. DeMeo, and Steve Gibbons

Authors

Todd M. Wilson is a wildlife biologist, U.S. Department of Agriculture, Forest Service, Pacific Northwest Research Station, Forestry Sciences Laboratory, 3200 SW Jefferson Way, Corvallis, OR 97331; **Reid Schuller** is a plant ecologist, Western Stewardship Science Institute, P.O. Box 1173, Bend, OR 97709; **Russ Holmes** is a regional botanist and **Thomas E. DeMeo** is a regional ecologist, U.S. Department of Agriculture, Forest Service, Pacific Northwest Region, 333 SW First Avenue, Portland, OR 97204; **Curt Pavola** is Program Manager, Natural Areas Program, Washington Department of Natural Resources, 1111 Washington Street SE, Olympia, WA 98504-7016; **Robert A. Fimbel** is Chief of Natural Resources Stewardship, Washington State Parks and Recreation Commission, 1111 Israel Rd., Olympia, WA 98504; **Cynthia N. McCain** is an ecologist, U.S. Department of Agriculture, Forest Service, Siuslaw and Willamette National Forests, P.O. Box 1148, Corvallis, OR 97339-1148; **John G. Gamon** is Program Manager of the Natural Heritage Program, Washington Department of Natural Resources, 1111 Washington Street SE, Olympia, WA 98504-7016; **Pene Speaks** is Assistant Division Manager, Washington Department of Natural Resources, Land Management Division, 1111 Washington Street SE, P.O. Box 47016, Olympia, WA 98504-7016; **Joan I. Seevers** is a state botanist, U.S. Department of the Interior, Bureau of Land Management, Oregon and Washington State Office, 333 SW First Avenue, Portland, OR 97204; **Steve Gibbons** is a natural resource specialist, National Park Service, Pacific West Region, 810 State Route 20, Sedro Woolley, WA 98284.

Cover photo: Mount Si Natural Resources Conservation Area, Washington Department of Natural Resources. Photo by Kelly Heintz.

Interagency Strategy for the Pacific Northwest Natural Areas Network

Todd M. Wilson, Reid Schuller, Russ Holmes, Curt Pavola, Robert A. Fimbel, Cynthia N. McCain, John G. Gamon, Pene Speaks, Joan I. Seevers, Thomas E. DeMeo, and Steve Gibbons

U.S. Department of Agriculture, Forest Service

Pacific Northwest Research Station

Portland, Oregon

General Technical Report PNW-GTR-798

July 2009

Published in cooperation with U.S. Department of the Interior, Bureau of Land Management, Oregon State Office; Washington Department of Natural Resources; and U.S. Forest Service, Pacific Northwest Region

Abstract

Wilson, Todd M.; Schuller, Reid; Holmes, Russ; Pavola, Curt; Fimbel, Robert A.; McCain, Cynthia N.; Gamon, John G.; Speaks, Pene; Seevers, Joan I.; DeMeo, Thomas E.; Gibbons, Steven. 2009. Interagency strategy for the Pacific Northwest Natural Areas Network. Gen. Tech. Rep. PNW-GTR-798. Portland, OR: U.S. Department of Agriculture, Forest Service, Pacific Northwest Research Station. 33 p.

Over the past 30 years, the Pacific Northwest Interagency Natural Areas Committee has promoted the establishment and management of natural areas in Oregon and Washington—protected areas devoted to research, education, and conservation of biodiversity. This growing collection of sites is now unmatched in its diversity and representation of both common and unique natural ecosystems found throughout this region. This strategy identifies visions, goals, and actions that can help transform this regional collection of natural areas into a network that has the resiliency to meet a growing number of challenges across five emphasis areas—inventory and designation, management, research, monitoring and data management, and education and communication. These challenges include managing for natural ecological processes over the long term, responding appropriately to threats such as climate change and invasive species, protecting the ecological integrity of sites as human use increases, promoting research and educational activities that address contemporary management issues, and communicating the importance of wildlands to a public that is growing apart from the natural world. Natural areas have the potential to serve as a critical network of sites for studying and developing regional and global approaches to conservation that meet diverse human and ecological needs, including managing for climate change.

Keywords: Natural areas, research natural area, biodiversity, ecological network, research properties, climate change.

Introduction

Lost Lake Research Natural Area, Bureau of Land Management, Medford District, Oregon.

Natural areas[1] are tracts of wildlands designated for research, education, and conservation purposes. As ecosystems in relatively pristine condition, they are managed primarily for their natural ecological processes, and in some cases, to help protect rare or threatened species. Natural areas range in size from tens of acres to several thousand acres. Collectively, they represent the wide gradient of ecosystems found throughout the Pacific Northwest. A number of government agencies and private organizations (hereafter, agencies) have formally established natural areas in Oregon and Washington (table 1).

Natural areas serve several critical functions. First, because they represent diverse terrestrial and aquatic ecosystems found in the region, they serve as foundations for several regional conservation strategies (Floberg et al. 2004, Iachetti et al. 2006, The Nature Conservancy 2000, Popper et al. 2007, Pryce et al. 2006, Raphael and Molina 2007, Vander Schaaf et al. 2006). They are also a subset of larger state, federal, and organizational efforts to protect important ecosystems across the globe (e.g., LandScope 2009, PAD-US 2009). This role is becoming increasingly important given the continued loss of wildlands from environmental

Natural areas serve as foundations for several regional conservation strategies.

---

[1] Agencies and organizations use a variety of terms to describe natural areas, including research natural area, area of critical environmental concern, natural area preserve, natural resource conservation area, biological study area, natural heritage conservation area, and natural area.

Table 1—Ownership and management of formally established natural areas in Oregon and Washington

	Number of sites	Total area	
		Acres	*Hectares*
Federal:			
U.S. Forest Service	81	101,826	41 208
Bureau of Land Management	101	276,866	112 044
National Park Service	15	31,380	12 699
U.S. Fish and Wildlife Service	19	37,505	15 178
U.S. Army	5	3,779	1 529
U.S. Army Corps of Engineers	2	178	72
U.S. Navy	1	5,177	2 095
Department of Energy	1	77,000	31 161
State:			
Oregon Department of State Lands	13	8,551	3 460
Oregon Parks and Recreation Department	36	14,893	6 027
Oregon Department of Fish and Wildlife	2	6,317	2 556
Washington Department of Natural Resources	84	158,408	64 105
Washington Department of Fish and Wildlife	6	10,950	4 431
Washington Parks and Recreation Commission	5	1,351	547
Washington State University	3	344	139
County:			
Benton County, Oregon	1	144	58
Lane County, Oregon	1	2,300	931
City:			
Metro (Portland-area regional government)	5	275	111
Private:			
The Nature Conservancy/other	79	168,632	68 243
Columbia Land Trust	2	158	64
Total	462	906,034	366 658

Note: Ownerships and values are approximate as of 2008. Data were obtained from multiple sources including state heritage plans and agency geographic information system layers, and are revised regularly owing to ongoing acquisitions, land ownership exchanges, and new formal designations or registrations with state heritage programs.
Source: ONHP 2003, WDRN 2007, unpublished data.

> **Natural areas can serve as controls for research studies, baselines for management activities, and living laboratories for education.**

degradation, fragmentation, and permanent conversion of land for other human uses. Second, natural areas are managed for their natural processes and therefore can serve as controls for research studies, baselines for management activities, and living laboratories for education. Third, as protected sites, natural areas provide a range of necessary ecological services for humans, including carbon sequestration, air and water filtration, water supply and regulation, erosion and sediment control, and local climate regulation. Finally, natural areas hold aesthetic, cultural, and intrinsic values that contribute to an increase in the quality of life for humans (Thompson and Starzomski 2007, Wilson 1984). These values are at risk of being lost because of a changing human demographic that is becoming increasingly disconnected from the natural world (Louv 2005, Pergams and Zaradic 2008).

The Pacific Northwest Interagency Natural Area Committee has been working together since the late 1960s to promote the recognition, establishment, and management of natural areas throughout Oregon and Washington. The committee currently comprises individuals representing 8 federal agencies; 10 state, county, and city agencies; and 2 nongovernmental organizations (table 1). One of the first committee projects was to identify key components of a multiagency, natural areas program (Dyrness et al. 1975). This led to the development of state heritage plans that used statewide inventories of wildlands to identify missing representations of ecosystems in the program (ONHP 2003, WDNR 2007). In 1991, the committee produced a set of guidelines for writing management and monitoring plans for natural areas (Greene et al. 1991). As a result of these and other efforts by natural resource professionals across the region, the natural areas program today has grown to over 400 sites spanning over 900,000 acres (367 000 ha), eclipsed only by wilderness and national parks for areas set aside to protect wildlands (table 1).

The point has now been reached where a cohesive network strategy may be needed to realize the full range of potential benefits from the natural areas program. There are several justifications for taking a cooperative approach to developing such a network. First, a growing number of land management issues cross ownership boundaries. A shared strategy allows opportunity for developing efficient and proactive approaches for dealing with environmental threats including catastrophic fire, invasive species, insect outbreaks, and climate change.

Second, an interagency network can capitalize on the collective experience that has resulted from developing agency-specific natural areas programs. Sharing resources and expert staffs can reduce costs associated with accomplishing similar objectives, and provide credibility that can help strengthen internal agency support. This is becoming increasingly important as agencies face shrinking budgets for establishing, monitoring, and maintaining natural areas.

Metolius Research Natural Area, Deschutes National Forest, Oregon.

Third, there is growing recognition that conservation efforts must be planned and implemented at varied spatial and temporal scales (Lindenmayer and Franklin 2002, Soulé and Terborgh 1999, Wiens 1989). Today, most natural areas are managed on a site-by-site basis with the intent to preserve ecosystems in perpetuity. However, all ecosystems will change over time as a consequence of natural processes and anthropogenic influences, regardless of management actions (Cole et al. 2008). Site-specific focus also does not consider the need for connectivity and permeability across the landscape that allows for flow of organisms over time—political boundaries are not recognized by most organisms (Lovejoy 2006). Planning solely at an agency level is also a problem, given that ecosystem representation is limited by the geopolitical boundaries of each agency (figs. 1 and 2). Therefore, a shared network strategy at a hierarchy of levels (from local to global) may be the only long-term solution for ensuring that the richness of regional and global ecosystems persists over time.

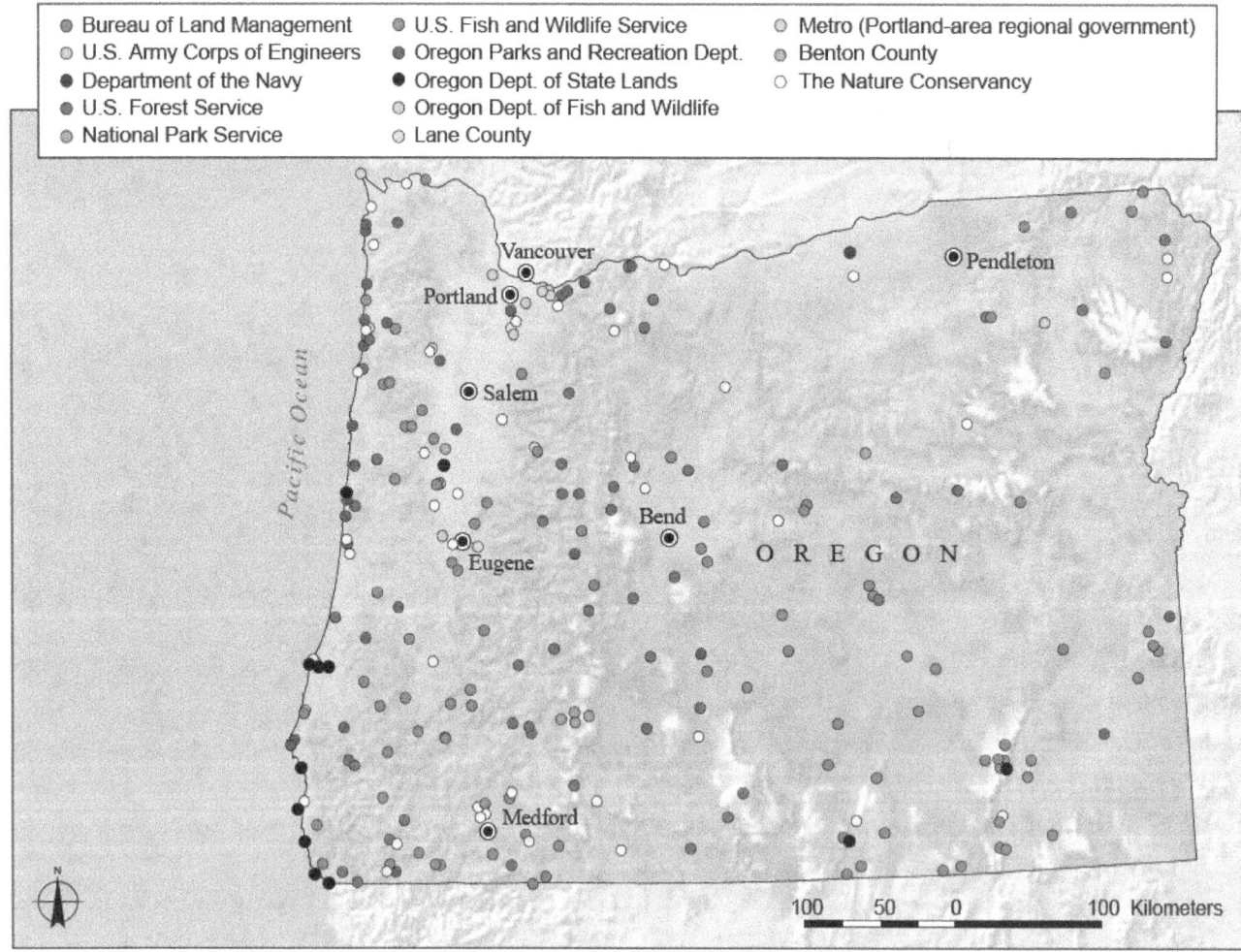

Figure 1—Formally established natural areas in Oregon as of December, 2008.

Purpose

The purpose of this document is to form the foundation of a strategy that can help turn the various natural areas programs in Oregon and Washington into a resilient network that is more strongly connected by shared agency objectives, management activities, research experiments, educational programs, and the continuum of ecosystems found across the region so that the full potential of these sites for meeting human and ecological needs can be realized. Five administrative areas are emphasized—inventory and designation, management, research, monitoring and data management, and education and communication. This strategy recognizes that no single agency has the capacity to represent or manage the diverse sites needed for comprehensive ecological representation, yet each agency has something valuable to contribute to the strength of the network. Common themes across emphasis areas include (1) use of partnerships and collaboration among agencies whenever

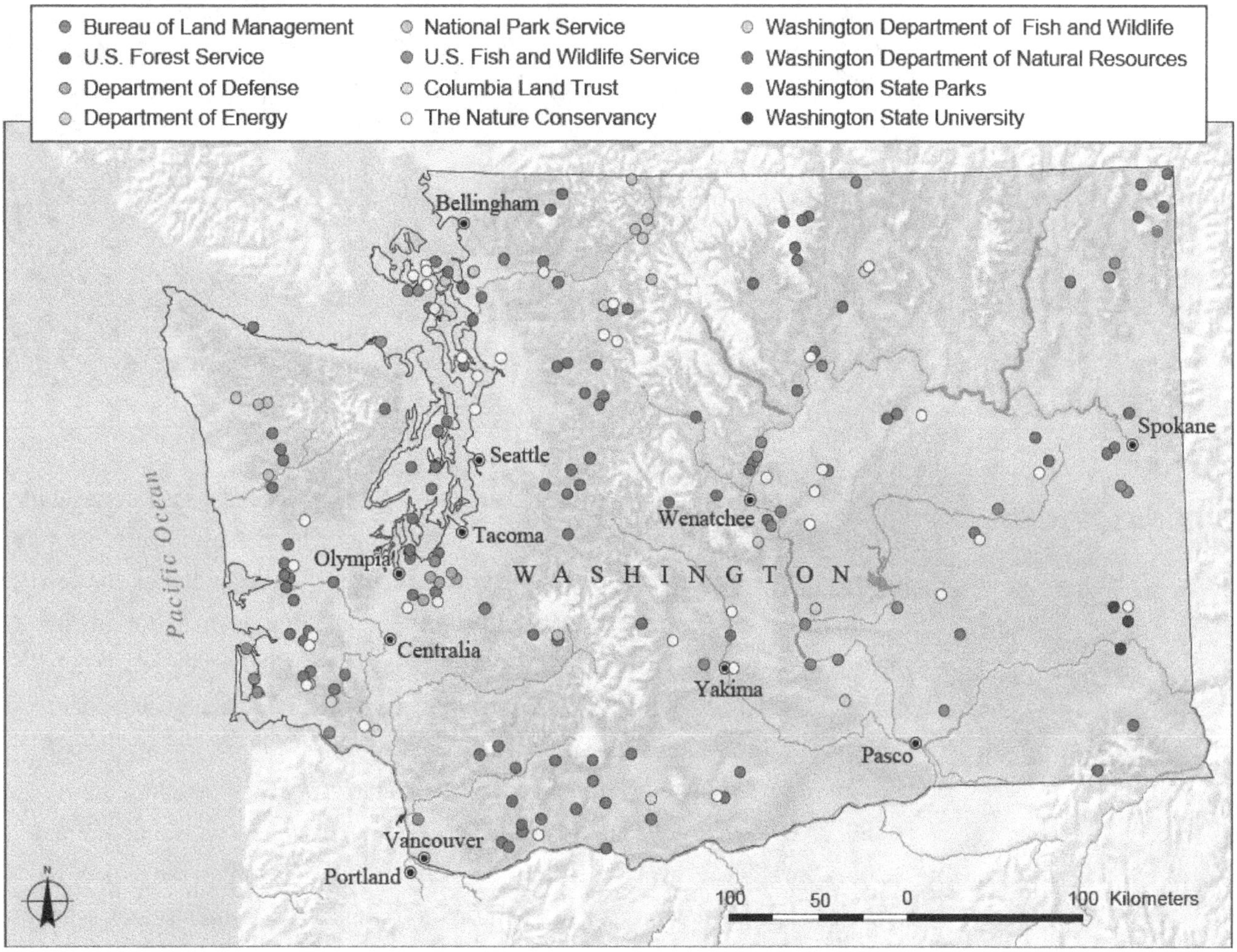

Figure 2—Formally established natural areas in Washington as of December, 2008.

possible in developing plans and carrying out strategic actions, (2) use of science as a basis for decisionmaking, (3) prioritizing tasks, and (4) seeking adequate internal and external support.

This strategy represents views of scientists and natural area professionals from a broad range of agencies and organizations in Oregon and Washington. However, it is not binding upon any of the participating agencies. This strategy should instead be viewed as an opportunity to meet individual agency missions by taking advantage of the synergy that can result from multiple groups working toward common

Bill Baccus

Twin Creek Research Natural Area, Olympic National Park, Washington.

goals, while still recognizing that constraints may be in place that restrict the ability of a given agency to achieve some of the goals outlined here. Additionally, meeting some goals may require changes in current agency procedures, protocols, or policies. In that case, this strategy may help provide compelling rationale for making such changes. It is also hoped that this strategy will be further developed over time and might stimulate thought for strengthening a national interagency network of natural areas both within and across agencies. Regardless of how this strategy is used, the desired outcome is a network of natural areas that can maintain high-quality ecosystems on the landscape that provide important ecological goods and services, meet the growing scientific and educational needs within the region, is resilient to human-induced change, and can accommodate natural changes over the long term.

I. Inventory and Designation

Vision

A network of natural areas is built that represents the full diversity of ecosystems found across the region while recognizing that each site is a dynamic ecosystem that will change over time.

Emerging Questions

- What should a "complete" natural areas network look like and what should the primary linkages be within this network?

- Can a network be designed in such a way that it is resilient to changes that will reshape these ecosystems over time?

Fitzner-Eberhardt Arid Lands Ecology Reserve, U.S. Department of Energy, Washington.

Inventory and Designation Goals

- ► Define and build a complete natural areas network for Oregon and Washington.

- ► Ensure that regional ecosystems and any associated rare species are represented in the natural areas network over the long term.

- ► Reduce institutional barriers to natural areas designation and access to establishment information.

- ► Improve establishment documentation.

Strategic Actions

- ► Complete establishment documentation, including up-to-date legal boundary descriptions, geographic information system maps, establishment reports, and guidebooks for both new and existing sites and establish a central file location accessible to all partners and interested publics (such as an interagency Web site).

- ► Add remaining missing ecosystems and species listed in current state heritage plans to the natural areas network, beginning with high-priority sites (ONHP 2003, WDNR 2007).

- ► Include proposed alternative sites, if available, when establishing a new natural area.

- ► Expand the scope of consideration for adding new natural areas to the network by collaborating with other agencies or other regional efforts to protect wildlands (e.g., CLC 2009, ODFW 2009, PSP 2009, SSI 2009).

- ► Conduct an interagency workshop focused on conceptual development of a complete natural areas network.

- ► Synthesize establishment information for each site and make this information available on public Web sites.

- ► Use land management planning processes as a tool for designating new natural areas.

- ► Incorporate mandatory state and federal environmental reviews for management in natural areas as part of broader agency planning efforts so that natural areas do not need to be addressed separately.

Horse Ridge Research Natural Area, Bureau of Land Management, Prineville District, Oregon.

The combined efforts to designate natural areas in Oregon and Washington since 1934 have resulted in a large number of formally established sites, with numerous additional sites being proposed (table 1, figs. 1 and 2). However, not all ecosystems found across the region are represented in the network. Therefore, continued effort is needed to add additional sites. This includes using state heritage plans to find unrepresented ecosystems and considering new sites as part of the landscape-level agency management plan or plan revisions. Of highest priority are those ecosystems that are rare or especially at risk to human-induced threats, including areas where human population growth is the fastest, e.g., Puget lowland, Willamette Valley, Rogue Valley, or where conversion to agricultural lands has been extensive, e.g., Columbia River basin (ONHP 2003, WDNR 2007). Although natural areas need not be large to protect rare, relatively sessile species (e.g., tens of acres), setting aside adequate space for ecosystem-level representation generally requires much larger sites (e.g., hundred to thousands of acres), and these are becoming increasingly difficult to find in places where human development is extensive.

As part of designation efforts, further conceptual development may also be needed to determine the composition of sites that should be included in a complete and resilient network. Today, each natural area represents an ecosystem that is relatively unique within the network (even if common to the landscape), and based primarily on plant associations. This approach may not be sufficiently holistic, especially given the large variation in structural and biological complexity that can be found within many of the plant associations in the Pacific Northwest. Representation by plant association also does not ensure that sites represent fully functioning ecosystems or consider that these ecosystems are dynamic and will change over time.

One option is to build a redundant natural areas network, with multiple representations of each ecosystem along a gradient of ecological stages and conditions. Such a network would allow for natural change to occur on any given site over time, while still maintaining representation of the ecosystem elsewhere in the network. The network could also be expanded to include biodiversity "hotspots" such as sites with rare species or those that comprise unique compositions of taxa that are not adequately captured by plant associations.

Site redundancy may be especially important given the growing recognition that climate change (natural and anthropogenic) may pose the greatest challenge to long-term management of natural ecosystems (Malcolm et al. 2002). However, redundancy alone will not be adequate to protect some sites in the face of environmental change. For example, climate change will likely result in differential shifts in plant and wildlife communities along moisture and elevational gradients as each organism responds uniquely to environmental change (Lovejoy 2006). This will require thinking about landscape permeability for organisms over time. Thus, a natural areas network should also consider how landscape context and management activities that occur outside of natural areas will influence effects of environmental changes at each site over time.

Climate change requires thinking about landscape permeability for organisms over time.

The complexity of the establishment process itself and length of time it takes to get a site established can be an impediment to designation. In some cases, it has taken over two decades to get sites formally established. For some agencies, procedures have been greatly streamlined in recent years as a result of policy changes that have reduced the number of steps needed for designation. Delays have also resulted from determinations that a site is not suitable as a natural area during the establishment process (e.g., conflict with other land use designation). Designating multiple alternative sites during establishment can be useful in preventing such delays.

Part of a complete natural areas network is also an administrative framework that can provide accurate and organized metadata associated with each site, including formal establishment records, legal boundary descriptions, and maps. Although many sites have some form of establishment documentation, the completeness and quality of this information varies among sites and agencies. For example, several natural areas were delineated before modern survey equipment was available. As a result, boundary descriptions and maps are not always accurate, which may result in inappropriate management activities being conducted on the site, especially near the boundaries.

Goat Marsh Research Natural Area, Gifford Pinchot National Forest, Washington.

Finally, better access to data and metadata will be needed, especially for promoting the use of natural areas. Often this information is not available electronically or is scattered across a number of platforms (e.g., geographic information system [GIS] map overlays in one department, hard copy records of establishment reports in another department). Guidebooks or other documents that synthesize establishment information (including designation purpose, general ecological characteristics, species lists, maps, and directions) are useful for locating sites, screening sites as potential research study areas, and for planning educational activities like field trips. Such public documentation is currently available for about 25 percent of the federal natural areas (Franklin et al. 1972, USDA FS 2009b). A number of alternative formats for synthesizing and publishing this information on public Web sites also exist that can facilitate access to natural areas administrative information.

II. Management

Vision

An adaptive, intentional, and science-based approach to management results in a natural areas network that is resilient to threats and environmental changes that will take place over time.

Emerging Questions:

- Can natural areas be managed in such a way as to be resilient to future human and natural-caused changes?

- Can natural areas be managed to prevent or minimize inappropriate human use?

- Should natural processes solely determine future conditions or should some sites be held at a particular stage of ecological development to meet original establishment objectives in perpetuity?

Chewuch Research Natural Area, Okanogan National Forest, Washington.

Management Goals

- ► Use an interdisciplinary, adaptive, and intentional approach to make informed and well-documented management decisions.

- ► Respond to potentially catastrophic disturbance such as human-caused fire, invasive species, and insect or disease outbreaks in a way that meets long-term natural area goals.

- ► Minimize the impacts of humans on natural processes at each site, especially those with heavy use.

Strategic Actions

- ► Establish site-specific long-term management objectives and priorities for each natural area and complete management plans that include addressing relevant issues and threats.

- ► Review and update current management plans, especially those created several decades ago that lack contemporary science-based management objectives. Resurvey/reinventory these sites as appropriate.

- ► Develop a site-specific, network-wide response plan to potential threats such as fire, invasive species, and insect or disease outbreaks.

- ► Develop water management plans that help protect natural areas that contain aquatic systems that could be used in fighting fire.

- ► Develop a curriculum for training permanent and seasonal fire personnel that work in and around natural areas. Incorporate this curriculum into standardized interagency wildfire training.

- ► Identify ecological communities and species that are most likely to be sensitive to climate change, and target these sites for more intensive, regular monitoring (Lawler and Mathias 2007).

- ► Establish early detection and rapid response programs and conduct regular surveys for invasive species, including transportation routes leading to natural areas (USDA FS 2004). Create GIS maps of current invasive species on each site and in surrounding areas.

- ► Develop a sign program that can be used to identify site boundaries to minimize trespass issues and inform the public of the importance of these sites.

- ► Develop criteria and protocols for managing human use of natural areas, including research, education, and recreational use.

- Will there be a time when select exotic species are accepted as part of these systems?
- What weight should be given to current predictions for climate changes and how will this affect decisions for when and where to take management actions?
- Can sufficient resources be found to accomplish strategic actions and effectively manage natural areas?

Long-term management strategies for natural areas will need to be both adaptable and intentional. Restoration efforts might best focus on restoring ecological processes.

The ecosystems represented in the natural areas network today are the result of cumulative effects of both natural and anthropogenic influences over millennia. They are not "pristine" in the sense that they have never been influenced by humans, yet they do represent some of the best examples of ecosystems whose present conditions have been primarily formed by nonhuman ("natural") processes. They are also not static, in that these sites will continue to change over time owing to both natural and human influences. Scientific knowledge and perceptions of the natural world will also continue to evolve, as will social trends, public needs, and legislative and regulatory direction.

Thus, long-term management strategies will need to be both adaptable and intentional in responding to these ecological and social changes (Carey 2007). This includes forethought as to how these ecosystems should look and function over the long term (e.g., centuries), as well as consideration for the long-term consequences of management actions (or inactions) taken today. For some sites, this may mean leaving them to develop with little or no human intervention (e.g., old-growth rain forest). For other sites, there is growing recognition that "hands-off" management can have unintended negative consequences (e.g., long-term fire suppression of dry, interior forest), and restoration activities like prescribed fire or thinning may be needed to shift these sites back onto more natural ecological trajectories. These restoration efforts might best focus on restoring ecological processes, rather than a desired end-state or ecological stage. This is especially important given little precedent for understanding or managing for rapid environmental change (Callicott 2002, Millar 2008).

Llao Rock Research Natural Area, Crater Lake National Park, Oregon.

Mima Mounds Natural Area Preserve, Washington Department of Natural Resources.

At times, management will need to react to immediate threats like catastrophic human-induced fire or invasive species. Intentional, proactive planning for how best to respond for each site could help reduce some of the negative consequences and costs associated with making decisions on the spot, or case by case. For example, lack of a well-communicated fire response plan may lead to suppression activities that result in unnecessary damage to soils, vegetation, and aquatic systems. Likewise, lack of an early-detection plan for invasive species may lead to expensive control options that could have otherwise been avoided had the species been detected early.

Management will also need to address a growing number of environmental threats in the region (Gamon 2007). Of these, climate change may be the most pervasive management challenge—even small changes in climate patterns could affect a wide range of ecological interactions and ecosystem processes and result in local

The natural areas network could serve as an important foundation for studying and developing regional or even global approaches to managing for climate change.

extirpations of rare organisms (Joyce et al. 2008, Kappelle et al. 1999, Millar et al. 2007, Noss 2001). There is currently little scientific basis for how best to manage for climate change, and it will be important to understand and ultimately manage for climate change at a hierarchy of spatial and temporal scales, from individual organisms to global ecosystems (Mustin et al. 2007). A number of different strategies may also be required (Millar 2008). Given its ecological depth and distribution, the natural areas network could serve as an important foundation for studying and developing regional or even global approaches to managing for climate change.

Forest Peak Research Natural Area, Bureau of Land Management, Salem District, Oregon.

Future management strategies will also need to address appropriate uses of natural areas as human populations continue to increase in the region. This includes better understanding of the impacts of human activities on natural areas. A number of concerns have already arisen over off-road vehicle use, horseback riding, livestock grazing, harvesting wildland products like mushrooms and floral greens, hunting, fishing, and camping. Use is especially of concern for sites that have infrastructures such as trailheads, parking lots, or established camp sites that encourage human use. Misuse of sites may, in part, be the result of lack of knowledge or appreciation for the importance of natural areas. Thus, there is potential to reduce human-use impacts through public outreach, education, and greater on-the-ground presence.

III. Monitoring and Data Management

Vision

Monitoring data are ecologically driven, consistently collected to acceptable scientific standards across the network, stored and maintained properly, and form an integral part of a feedback loop for making and evaluating management decisions.

Emerging Questions

- Can baseline and monitoring protocols be developed and used across the entire natural areas network?

- Can a network-wide monitoring strategy be designed that will be useable over the long term?

- Can data be synergistically managed and shared across agencies?

Pringle Falls Research Natural Area, Deschutes National Forest, Oregon.

Monitoring and Data Management Goals

- ► To establish a monitoring program that is consistent in objectives, priorities, and protocols across the natural areas network.

- ► To collect monitoring data in a way that can provide both site-specific and network-wide evaluations.

- ► To provide long-term storage and accessibility of data.

- ► To use monitoring data to make informed decisions about the management of natural areas.

Strategic Actions

- ► Develop clearly defined site-specific and network-wide monitoring objectives that include timeframes and criteria for measuring monitoring success.

- ► Assess the utility of existing monitoring protocols and databases (including baseline documentation) in meeting contemporary management goals, likely future management challenges, and their ability to be combined with other long-term data sets.

- ► Determine the appropriate ecological indicators needed to measure changes to these systems and the surrounding landscape over time.

- ► Develop interagency monitoring protocols and databases that have the capacity to link with other monitoring and research databases through use of a centralized database and portal.

- ► Establish relocatable permanent plots for collecting data at each site.

- ► Establish a photographic point monitoring program for each site (Hall 2002).

- ► Collect visitor-use data at sites with potentially heavy human use, including purpose of visit, group size, date and length of visit, and affiliations.

- ► Develop protocols for proper data management that includes creating metadata associated with data sets, proper storage and archiving of data, and keeping up with changes in software and species nomenclature. This may require innovative database approaches that may be more suitable for scientific data (e.g., Pfaltz 2007), education, and recreational use.

The Island Research Natural Area, jointly administered by Bureau of Land Management, Prineville District, and Forest Service, Crooked River National Grassland, Oregon.

Collecting baseline and monitoring data provides a number of useful benefits for the long-term management of natural areas, including (1) site-specific data for making management decisions; (2) feedback on the effectiveness of mitigation, restoration, and offsite management activities; (3) inventory of the ecological characteristics of a site; (4) quantified assessment of natural and anthropogenic influences over time; (5) data for refining monitoring and management protocols; and (6) information for long-term scientific study of ecosystems and ecological processes.

A number of monitoring and data management issues will need to be resolved to strengthen the current monitoring program. First, ecological monitoring programs have been inconsistently established across the network (e.g., <20 percent of federal sites, >50 percent of state sites, but >75 percent of The Nature Conservancy sites). For those sites that are not monitored, information about the site is often limited to lists of plant and wildlife species expected to occur on these sites rather than actual inventories.

Second, where monitoring data are being collected, problems can range from different protocols being used across sites, divergence of protocols over time, lack of connection between data being collected and site management objectives, and irregular monitoring schedules once initial data have been collected. A long-term monitoring program with shared monitoring goals, diverse but consistent protocols to meet both site-specific and cross-site objectives, and regular monitoring schedules can increase sampling power, strengthen statistical inferences within and across sites, and ultimately provide empirical support for management actions both within and around natural areas.

Third, current monitoring data are primarily focused on vegetation and related composition. Opportunities exist for expanding monitoring programs to (1) capture a fuller gradient of multidimensional structural measures that evaluate broader ecological processes and (2) include a wider range of indicators that can measure ecological health and function over time owing to environmental change, including microclimate, assessments of key wildlife communities, nutrient cycling, soils, and carbon flux. This might also include measures that can evaluate changes in ecological processes rather than simply changes in the spatial distribution or abundance of select species or taxonomic groups (e.g., McIntire and Fajardo 2009). It could also include measuring changes to trophic hierarchies over time as we have little knowledge about where environmental change will have the greatest effects, or where it will have the first effects (e.g., at the top or bottom of a food chain) (Wagner and Adrian 2009).

Fourth, many of the strategies outlined here will result in increased use of natural areas. The risk in promoting use is that it could affect the environmental integrity of some sites, especially those that are sensitive to foot traffic, or sites that have established infrastructures that might already promote heavy use (e.g., parking areas, trails). Therefore, some form of monitoring focused on human-use effects may be needed to help preempt any long-term negative consequences that promoting additional use may have for some sites.

Finally, a cursory inquiry into data management strategies across agencies suggests that data for natural areas are not always handled in ways that ensure their long-term protection and use. Many data sets reside in unsecured boxes, have never been entered into an electronic database, or have no associated metadata to provide the necessary context for the data. Long-term data management requires a program that extends beyond the employment of individual administrators, can resurrect historical data, provides data access to the broader community, reduces time and effort spent searching for data, and allows for data to be used to address broad-scale questions (Michener and Brunt 2000).

Butter Creek Research Natural Area, Gifford Pinchot National Forest and Mount Rainier National Park, Washington.

Therese Ohlson

Wolf Creek Research Natural Area, Okanogan National Forest, Washington.

IV. Research

Vision

The depth of research conducted throughout the natural areas network contributes to the understanding and resolution of important scientific, social, and economic issues across a range of spatial and temporal scales.

High Peak/Moon Creek Research Natural Area, Bureau of Land Management, Salem District, Oregon.

Emerging Questions:

- Can researchers be encouraged to conduct more studies on and across natural areas, especially those sites that have received little use to date?

- Can research address questions and issues that will contribute to successful management of natural areas?

- Do management or restoration activities preclude the ability to study natural processes?

Research Goals

- ▶ Develop and promote awareness for using natural areas as research study sites.
- ▶ Make research results available to diverse audiences.
- ▶ Encourage research that addresses long-term management goals for the natural area as well as priority management issues.
- ▶ Improve documentation of the entire research process, from study proposal to final publication.

Strategic Actions

- ▶ Develop Web sites with sections devoted specifically to research that include search tools for species and ecological characteristics at each site and a comprehensive bibliography of all published research conducted across the natural area network.
- ▶ Convert journal-based research information into alternative formats that can reach broader audiences (e.g., synthesis papers, varied multimedia formats)
- ▶ Promote natural areas as satellite sites for existing national ecological networks.
- ▶ Establish consistent criteria for appropriate research use of natural areas, including standardized research application permits.

- ▶ Streamline the permitting and approval process for research requests, including the use of electronic submissions.
- ▶ Develop distribution lists for dissemination of natural areas research.
- ▶ Develop an electronic tracking system for documenting research use at natural areas, including consistent requirements for submitting research request materials, and followup strategies for reporting results and publications.
- ▶ Develop and maintain single-source electronic libraries of all research and monitoring projects.
- ▶ Present research results from natural areas in synthesis papers, annual reports, newsletters, and other agency communication outlets. Highlight especially those that lead to discovery of a new ecological concept, development of a new management approach, or assist in the understanding of a rare or threatened species.
- ▶ Use a team-room or "Facebook" style Web portal for storing research-related materials.
- ▶ Develop an interagency (or agency-rotating) research seed grant fund program for conducting studies on natural areas that address pressing management questions.

Research on natural areas may be one of the best ways to gain knowledge for addressing contemporary management and conservation issues.

A primary purpose for natural areas is to allow study of ecological processes that can improve our understanding of the natural world. Many of the issues facing conservation (climate change, invasive species, etc.) will require refinement of ecological theory and better understanding of ecological processes and function. Research on natural areas may be one of the best ways to gain this knowledge, especially given that they represent some of the most pristine, intact natural ecosystems left on the landscape.

Silver Lake Research Natural Area, North Cascades National Park, Washington.

A number of important research findings have been based on data collected from natural areas in the past, including studies of old-growth forest that helped lead to the Northwest Forest Plan, the set of documents that has guided management activities on federal lands since 1994 (USDA and USDI 1994). However, many natural areas have received little research attention (Greene et al. 1986). Reasons for lack of use are varied, including relative remoteness of sites from other research sites or centers of research, lack of site replication, some sites representing ecosystems not under current scientific scrutiny, and recent establishment for a number of sites. The lack of use has also been the result of unfamiliarity of researchers with the benefits of using natural areas and misconceptions over the types of appropriate research allowed on natural areas. Agencies have also differed in the degree to which they have actively encouraged or promoted research on natural areas. These reasons for lack of use suggest there is opportunity to better promote natural areas for research, both internally (within the home agency or organization) and externally to research clients.

There are a number of characteristics unique to the natural areas that make them attractive as study sites, especially for understanding ecological processes and effects of climate change: (1) They are geographically well-distributed throughout the region (figs. 1 and 2) representing almost the entire gradient of natural biophysical environments found in the Pacific Northwest. This includes gradients in soils, moisture, temperature, elevation, latitude, and other biotic and abiotic conditions. (2) They contain sites representing environmental extremes, including rare ecosystems that might be the most sensitive to change over time. (3) The biological diversity contained within natural areas allows for study at all hierarchical levels, from genes to individual organisms to complete communities and systems. (4) As relatively pristine sites, natural areas can be used as controls for nearby field experiments as well as benchmarks for measuring the efficacy of management activities (Julius and West 2008, Joyce et al. 2008). (5) Most natural areas are permanently protected, allowing for long-term study. A network strategy for climate change research could include everything from collecting climatological data at remote sensing stations to periodic field surveys of climate-sensitive organisms at permanent sampling plots using standardized protocols.

A network strategy for climate change research could include everything from collecting climatological data at remote sensing stations to periodic field surveys of climate-sensitive organisms.

Natural areas can also be promoted as satellite study sites in association with other major ecological networks and programs, including U.S. Forest Service experimental forests and ranges, wilderness areas, and national scenic rivers, Department of the Interior national parks and U.S. Geological Survey Hydrologic Benchmark Network program, United Nations Biosphere Reserves, the Long-Term Ecological Research (LTER) Network, the National Ecological Observatory Network (NEON), Long-Term Ecosystem Productivity forestry research network, and the National Atmospheric Deposition and National Acid Precipitation Assessment Programs.

As with management and monitoring, research use of natural areas can be enhanced through dedicated funding, either as a regular component of annual agency budgets, or through funding of special projects. For example, seed grants to graduate students could help

Hat Island Natural Resources Conservation Area, Washington Department of Natural Resources.

promote collaborative research with academic institutions. Increased support for research can also be generated by better communication of research studies and their results. This includes better documentation for past and ongoing research projects, encouraging cradle-to-grave research projects to ensure that results are actually published, and communicating results in different ways to meet the needs of diverse audiences that have an interest in resource management.

Grass Mountain Research Natural Area, Bureau of Land Management, Salem District, Oregon.

Using natural areas to build stronger ties between research and management can help strengthen the importance and relevance of research on natural areas.

Finally, using natural areas to build stronger ties between research and management can help strengthen the importance and relevance of research on natural areas. For example, a number of restoration projects, including woody fuels reduction, prescribed fire, and invasive species control are being proposed for natural areas. However, there is little information available on the site-specific efficacy of these tools, including how they might affect future ecological processes. Close coordination between research and management in designing studies that evaluate these restoration efforts could provide important feedback that results in better management in and around natural areas, and greater appreciation for the importance of research on these sites.

V. Education and Communication

Vision

Education and communication activities connect people with nature, promote understanding of ecology and conservation, increase volunteerism, and strengthen agency and public support for the natural areas network.

Emerging Questions:

- Can the overall potential negative ecological impacts from increased use of natural areas be reduced or eliminated through increased education, participation, and support by the public?

- How should internal support for the natural areas network best be strengthened?

Limpy Rock Research Natural Area, Umpqua National Forest, Oregon.

Education and Communication Goals

- ▶ Increase internal and external support for the natural areas network.
- ▶ Provide better access to natural areas for the purposes of conservation, education, and connection with nature.
- ▶ Encourage broader use of natural areas by those from both traditional environment-related sciences and other disciplines (arts and humanities).

Strategic Actions

- ▶ Develop an educational strategy for targeting K-12 students. This may include coordinating activities between agencies and zoos, schools, and environmental education institutions that have existing educational programs.
- ▶ Develop a marketing and communications plan for encouraging the education use of natural areas.
- ▶ Create posters and pamphlets with key messages to specific target audiences.
- ▶ Develop and provide natural areas network literature to colleges and K-12 instititutions. Include natural resources, sciences, and environmental education departments as well as arts and humanities departments.

- ▶ Develop a volunteer program that includes plans for administration, marketing, evaluation, and supervision (Flood et al. 2006). Collaborate with existing volunteer programs where possible.
- ▶ Organize workshops around natural areas that bring artists, educators, and the public together to develop a sense of place and connection with nature.
- ▶ Partner with citizen groups, professional organizations (such as the Natural Areas Association), nonprofit organizations, educators, and local communities to assist with monitoring, management, and educational outreach.
- ▶ Promote natural areas as places for learning with environmental institutes and nature study centers.
- ▶ Initiate pilot projects for using natural areas as a setting for mentoring youth.
- ▶ Target education and information sections of interagency Web sites to a wide range of students and the general public.
- ▶ Promote natural areas information and success stories to local and regional news media.

Part of a strong interagency network includes effective education, communication, and outreach programs. Regional natural areas have been available as outdoor educational laboratories since their inception. Overall use of natural areas as sites for educational activities, however, has been relatively low.

There is opportunity to expand the scope of educational activities to include a focus on younger students.

Sheep Rock Research Natural Area, John Day Fossil Beds National Monument, National Park Service, Oregon.

Most natural area educational programs to date have focused on educating college-level and higher students, professional societies, and special-interest groups. There is opportunity to expand the scope of educational activities to include a focus on younger (e.g., K-12) students. Recent social trends in the United States suggest that youth may no longer be getting sufficient exposure to the outdoors, and encounters with nature can help reduce aggression, calm anxiety, and develop a healthy sense of self and place (Pilz et al. 2006). A number of agencies have recently added youth education as a top emphasis area (e.g., Kimbell 2009). Engaging youth can also help promote a future adult population that is environmentally literate and appreciates the importance of natural areas and wildlands (USDA FS 2009a).

Opportunities also exist for expanding the scope of disciplines associated with the use of natural areas beyond traditional science-based fields. For example, individuals from the arts and humanities are increasingly using wildlands as settings for their nature writing, painting, or other forms of artistic expression (e.g., SCAE 2009). Fostering such use on natural areas can help build a constituency that appreciates and supports natural areas.

Support can also be fostered within local communities near natural areas by developing volunteer and citizen science programs to assist with research, monitoring, site surveillance, restoration projects, and community outreach (Lowman et al. 2009, Yung 2007). Many of the strategic actions presented here can be supported, in part, through the use of volunteers. Volunteers are not free in terms of the amount of staff time needed for recruitment, training, and oversight. However, the benefits of incorporating their efforts can often outweigh these costs, and they offer an alternative for accomplishing tasks, especially when budgets are limited. A number of partners, supporters, and target groups could be considered (table 2).

There is also need for increasing the understanding and appreciation of natural areas within the agencies that manage them. There are still a number of misconceptions about natural areas—for example, that natural areas are small, unique pieces of land set aside solely to protect an unusual ecosystem. In part, these misconceptions have arisen because information about natural areas is often site-specific (establishment of a single site, result from a single study). These misperceptions also result when the importance of natural areas is not being

Many of the strategic actions presented here can be supported, in part, through the use of volunteers.

Table 2—Potential partners, supporters, and citizen groups that could assist with management and monitoring efforts for natural areas in the Pacific Northwest

Professional ecological, wildlife, native plant, forestry, and range societies
Watershed councils
Youth conservation corps
Local and regional land trusts
Natural history institutes
Private land-managing conservation organizations
Fish and wildlife citizen groups
Grange organizations
Outdoor user recreational groups
Youth clubs
Gardening clubs
Master gardeners
Master naturalists
Local media (newspapers/TV/radio stations)
Community education programs
"Friends of" groups
Local governments—planners
Advocacy organizations
Federal, state, or local foundations and councils
Outdoor equipment and supply stores
Senior centers
State and county noxious weed programs
Local libraries
Public service organizations
Current and past agency employees and volunteers

effectively translated from the field (where most natural area information is generated) in ways that resonate with upper-level management. Therefore, strategic actions include those that can frame information in ways that show network-level strength and that can be directly tied to support of agency missions. These could include highlighting (1) cost-savings associated with managing natural areas as a network across sites and agencies; (2) important findings from natural areas that increase knowledge for making sound management decisions; (3) the strength of connections with other agencies, partners, and organizations that resulted from participating in the natural areas network; (4) increased public support of management activities as a result of natural areas management or research; (5) the importance of natural areas for providing high-quality sites for research; and (6) broad biodiversity and conservation goals met by natural areas.

Little Wildhorse Research Natural Area, Steens Mountain Cooperative Management and Protection Area, Bureau of Land Management, Burns District, Oregon.

Acknowledgments

Many of the ideas for this strategy arose from the 45+ participants who attended the Pacific Northwest Interagency Natural Areas Committee workshop for natural areas professionals held October 9–10, 2007, in Corvallis, Oregon. Additional input was received during indepth interviews with selected natural area professionals and research scientists. T. Valentine provided GIS support. Helpful review comments were provided by S. Greene, T. Mowrer, M. Peterson, and S. Shelly. This project was jointly funded by the Department of the Interior, Bureau of Land Management; Washington Department of Natural Resources; and U.S. Department of Agriculture, Forest Service, Region 6 and Pacific Northwest Research Station.

Pyramid Lake Research Natural Area, North Cascades National Park, Washington.

Metric Equivalent

When you know:	Multiply by:	To find:
Acres	0.405	Hectares (ha)

Literature Cited

Callicott, J.B. 2002. Choosing appropriate temporal and spatial scales for ecological restoration. Journal of Bioscience. 27(4): 409–420.

Carey, A.B. 2007. AIMing for healthy forests: active, intentional management for multiple values. Gen. Tech. Rep. PNW-GTR-721. Portland, OR: U.S. Department of Agriculture, Forest Service, Pacific Northwest Research Station. 447 p.

Cascade Land Conservancy [CLC]. 2009. Cascade agenda: great lands, great communities. http://www.cascadeagenda.com/. (10 March 2009).

Cole, D.N.; Yung, L.; Zavaleta, E.S.; Aplet, G.H.; Chapin, F.S., III; Graber, D.M.; Higgs, E.S.; Hobbs, R.J.; Landres, P.B.; Millar, C.I.; Parsons, D.J.; Randall, J.M.; Stephenson, N.L.; Tonnessen, K.A.; White, P.S.; Woodley, S. 2008. Naturalness and beyond: protected area stewardship in an era of global environmental change. The George Wright Forum. 25(1): 36–56.

Dyrness, C.T.; Franklin, J.F.; Maser, C.; Cook, S.A.; Hall, J.D.; Faxon, G. 1975. Research natural area needs in the Pacific Northwest: a contribution to land-use planning. Gen. Tech. Rep. PNW-38. Portland, OR: U.S. Department of Agriculture, Forest Service, Pacific Northwest Forest and Range Experiment Station. 231 p.

Floberg, J.; Goering, M.; Wilhere, G.; MacDonald, C.; Chappell, C.; Rumsey, C.; Ferdana, Z.; Holt, A.; Skidmore, P.; Horsman, T.; Alverson, E.; Tanner, C.; Bryer, M.; Iachetti, P.; Harcombe, A.; McDonald, B.; Cook, T.; Summers, M.; Rolph, D. 2004. Willamette Valley-Puget Trough-Georgia Basin ecoregional assessment. Volume 1. Report. Prepared by The Nature Conservancy with support from the Nature Conservancy of Canada, Washington Department of Fish and Wildlife, Washington Department of Natural Resources (Natural Heritage and Nearshore Habitat programs), Oregon State Natural Heritage Information Center, and the British Columbia Conservation Data Centre. http://hdl.handle.net/1957/57. (7 June 2009).

Flood, J.P.; Gardner, E.; Yarrell, K. 2006. Managing volunteers: developing and implementing an effective program. In: Peden, J.G.; Schuster, R.M., comps., eds. Proceedings of the 2005 northeastern recreation research symposium. Gen. Tech. Rep. NE-341. Newtown Square, PA: U.S. Department of Agriculture, Forest Service, Northeastern Research Station: 80–88.

Franklin, J.F.; Hall, F.C.; Dyrness, C.T.; Maser, C. 1972. Federal research natural areas in Oregon and Washington. Portland, OR: U.S. Department of Agriculture, Forest Service, Pacific Northwest Forest and Range Experiment Station. [No pagination].

Gamon, J. 2007. Washington's biodiversity: status and threats. Olympia, WA: Washington Biodiversity Council. 51 p.

Greene, S.E.; Blinn, T.; Franklin, J.F. 1986. Research natural areas in Oregon and Washington: past and current research and related literature. Gen. Tech. Rep. PNW-GTR-197. Portland, OR: U.S. Department of Agriculture, Forest Service, Pacific Northwest Research Station. 115 p.

Greene, S.E.; McDonald, C.; Schuller, R. 1991. Sourcebook for natural area coordinators. Unpublished report. On file with: USDA Forest Service, Pacific Northwest Research Station, 3200 Jefferson Way, Corvallis, OR 97331. [No pagination].

Hall, F.C. 2002. Photo point monitoring handbook—Part A: field procedures; Part B: concepts and analysis. Gen. Tech. Rep. PNW-GTR-526. Portland, OR: U.S. Department of Agriculture, Forest Service, Pacific Northwest Research Station. 48 p.

Iachetti, P.; Floberg, J.; Wilhere, G.; Ciruna, K.; Markovic, D.; Lewis, J.; Heiner, M.; Kittel, G.; Crawford, R.; Farone, S.; Ford, S.; Goering, M.; Nicolson, D.; Tyler, S.; Skidmore, P. 2006. North Cascades and Pacific Ranges ecoregional assessment. Volume 1. Report. Prepared by the Nature Conservancy of Canada, The Nature Conservancy of Washington, and the Washington Department of Fish and Wildlife with support from the British Columbia Conservation Data Centre, Washington Department of Natural Resources Natural Heritage Program, and NatureServe. Victoria, BC: Nature Conservancy of Canada. 85 p.

Joyce, L.A.; Blate, G.M.; Littell, J.S.; McNulty, S.G.; Millar, C.I.; Moser, S.C.; Neilson, R.P.; O'Halloran, K.; Peterson, D.L.; Scott, J.M. 2008. National forests. In: Julius, S.H.; West, J.M., eds. Preliminary review of adaptation options for climate-sensitive ecosystems and resources. A report by the U.S. Climate Change Science Program and the Subcommittee on Global Change Research. Washington, DC: U.S. Environmental Protection Agency: 3-1 to 3-127. http://www.climatescience.gov/Library/sap/sap4-4/final-report/default.htm. (28 June 2009).

Julius, S.H.; West, J.M., eds. 2008. Preliminary review of adaptation options for climate-sensitive ecosystems and resources. A report by the U.S. Climate Change Science Program and the Subcommittee on Global Change Research. Washington, DC: U.S. Environmental Protection Agency. 873 p.

Kappelle, M.; Van Vuuren, M.M.I.; Bass, P. 1999. Effects of climate change on biodiversity: a review and identification of key research issues. Biodiversity and Conservation. 8(10): 1383–1397.

Kimbell, A.R. 2009. Climate change, water, and kids. http://www.fs.fed.us/emphasis/. (4 March 2009).

LandScope. 2009. Landscope America: the conservation guide to America's natural places. http://www.landscope.org/. (27 May 2009).

Lawler, J.J.; Mathias, M. 2007. Climate change and the future of biodiversity in Washington. Report prepared for the Washington Biodiversity Council. 42 p. http://www.biodiversity.wa.gov/documents/WA-CC-report-final.pdf. (28 July 2009).

Lindenmayer, D.; Franklin, J.F. 2002. Conserving forest biodiversity: a comprehensive multiscaled approach. Washington, DC: Island Press. 368 p.

Louv, R. 2005. Last child in the woods: saving our children from nature-deficit disorder. Chapel Hill, NC: Algonquin Books of Chapel Hill. 336 p.

Lovejoy, T.E. 2006. Protected areas: a prism for a changing world. Trends in Ecology and Evolution. 21(6): 329–333.

Lowman, M.; D'Avanzo, C.; Brewer, C. 2009. A national ecological network for research and education. Science. 323: 1172–1173.

Malcolm, J.R.; Liu, C.; Miller, L.B.; Allnutt, T.; Hansen, L. 2002. Habitats at risk: global warming and species loss in globally significant terrestrial ecosystems. Gland, Switzerland: World Wildlife Fund for Nature. 39 p.

McIntire, E.J.B.; Fajardo, A. 2009. Beyond description: the active and effective way to infer processes from spatial patterns. Ecology. 90(1): 46–56.

Michener, W.K.; Brunt, J.W., eds. 2000. Ecological data: design, management and processing (ecological methods and concepts). Hoboken, NJ: Wiley-Blackwell. 192 p.

Millar, C.I. 2008. Natural resource strategies and climate change. U.S. Department of Agriculture, Forest Service, Climate Change Resource Center. http://www.fs.fed.us/ccrc/topics/natural-resource.shtml. (16 June 2008).

Millar, C.I.; Stephenson, N.L.; Stephens, S.L. 2007. Climate change and forests of the future: managing in the face of uncertainty. Ecological Applications. 17(8): 2145–2151.

Mustin, K.; Sutherland, W.J.; Gill, J.A. 2007. The complexity of predicting climate-induced ecological impacts. Climate Research. 35: 165–175.

The Nature Conservancy. 2000. Middle Rockies–Blue Mountains ecoregional conservation plan. Arlington, VA. 57 p. + appendices.

Noss, R.F. 2001. Beyond Kyoto: forest management in a time of rapid climate change. Conservation Biology. 15: 578–590.

Oregon Department of Fish and Wildlife [ODFW]. 2009. Oregon conservation strategy. http://www.dfw.state.or.us/conservationstrategy/index.asp. (9 January 2009).

Oregon Natural Heritage Program [ONHP]. 2003. Oregon natural heritage plan. Salem, OR: Department of State Lands. 167 p. http://oregonstate.edu/ornhic/ documents/ornh_plan.pdf. (7 July 2009).

Pergams, O.R.W.; Zaradic, P.A. 2008. Evidence for a fundamental and pervasive shift away from nature-based recreation. Proceedings of the National Academy of Sciences. Palo Alto, CA: Stanford University. DOI: 10.1073/pnas.0709893105.

Pfaltz, J.L. 2007. What constitutes a scientific database? 19th international conference on scientific and statistical database management. Washington, DC: IEEE Computer Society: 2.

Pilz, D.; Ballard, H.L.; Jones, E.T. 2006. Broadening participation in biological monitoring: handbook for scientists and managers. Gen. Tech. Rep. PNW-GTR-680. Portland, OR: U.S. Department of Agriculture, Forest Service, Pacific Northwest Research Station. 131 p.

Popper, K.; Wilhere, G.; Schindel, M.; Vander Schaaf, D.; Skidmore, P.; Stroud, G.; Crandall, J.; Kagan, J.; Crawford, R.; Kittel, G.; Azerrad, J.; Bach, L. 2007. The East Cascades–Modoc Plateau and the West Cascades ecoregional assessments. Prepared by The Nature Conservancy and the Washington Department of Fish and Wildlife with support from the Oregon Natural Heritage Information Center, Washington Heritage Program, and NatureServe. Portland, OR: The Nature Conservancy. http://www. waconservation.org/ecoWestCascades.shtml. (7 July 2009).

Protected Areas Database of the United States (PAD-US). 2009. http://protectedlands.net/main/home.php (23 May 2009).

Pryce, B.; Iachetti, P.; Wilhere, G.; Ciruna, K.; Floberg, J.; Crawford, R.; Dye, R.; Fairbarns, M.; Farone, S.; Ford, S.; Goering, M.; Heiner, M.; Kittel, G.; Lewis, J.; Nicolson, D.; Warner, N. 2006. Okanagan ecoregional assessment. Volume 1. Report. Prepared by Nature Conservancy of Canada, The Nature Conservancy of Washington, and the Washington Department of Fish and Wildlife with support from the British Columbia Conservation Data Centre, Washington Department of Natural Resources Natural Heritage Program, and NatureServe. Victoria, BC: Nature Conservancy of Canada. http://science.natureconservancy.ca/resources/resources_w.php?pageNum_ rsResources=3&Type=all&Region=all&Key=okanagan+ecoregion&totalRows_ rsResources=41. (7 July 2009).

Puget Sound Partnership [PSP]. 2009. Puget Sound Partnership: our sound, our community, our chance. http://www.psp.wa.gov. (11 January 2009).

Raphael, M.G.; Molina, R., eds. 2007. Conservation of rare or little-known species: biological, social, and economic considerations. Washington, DC: Island Press. 375 p.

Sitka Center for Art and Ecology [SCAE]. 2009. Sitka Center for Art and Ecology home page. http://www.sitkacenter.org. (4 March 2009).

Soulé, M.E.; Terborgh, J. 1999. Continental conservation: scientific foundation of regional reserve networks. Washington, DC: Island Press. 227 p.

Sustainable Sites Initiative [SSI]. 2009. The Sustainable Sites Initiative home page. http://www.sustainablesites.org. (7 July 2009).

Thompson, R.; Starzomski, B.M. 2007. What does biodiversity actually do? A review for managers and policy makers. Biodiversity and Conservation. 16: 1359–1378.

U.S. Department of Agriculture, Forest Service [USDA FS]. 2004. National strategy and implementation plan for invasive species management. FS-805. Washington, DC. 17 p.

U.S. Department of Agriculture, Forest Service [USFS]. 2009a. Kids in the woods. http://www.fs.fed.us/emphasis/kids.shtml. (6 March 2009).

U.S. Department of Agriculture, Forest Service [USDA FS]. 2009b. USFS research publications. http://www.treesearch.fs.fed.us/. (16 March 2009).

U.S. Department of Agriculture, Forest Service; U.S. Department of the Interior, Bureau of Land Management [USDA and USDI]. 1994. Final supplemental environmental impact statement on management of habitat for late-successional and old-growth forest related species within the range of the northern spotted owl. Volumes 1–2 + Record of Decision, Portland, OR.

Vander Schaaf, D.; Wilhere, G.; Ferdaña, Z.; Popper, K.; Schindel, M.; Skidmore, P.; Rolph, D.; Iachetti, P.; Kittel, G.; Crawford, R.; Pickering, D.; Christy, J. 2006. Pacific Northwest Coast Ecoregion Assessment. Prepared by The Nature Conservancy, the Nature Conservancy of Canada, and the Washington Department of Fish and Wildlife. Portland, OR: The Nature Conservancy. http://hdl.handle.net/1957/4638. (26 March 2009).

Wagner, C.; Adrian, R. 2009. Exploring lake ecosystems: hierarchy responses to long-term changes? Global Change Biology. 15: 1104–1115.

Washington Department of Natural Resources [WDNR]. 2007. State of Washington Natural Heritage Plan 2007. Olympia, WA. 100 p. http://www1.dnr.wa.gov/nhp/refdesk/plan/index.html. (11 January 2009).

Wiens, J.A. 1989. Spatial scaling in ecology. Functional Ecology. 3: 385–397.

Wilson, E.O. 1984. Biophilia. Cambridge, MA: Harvard University Press. 176 p.

Yung, L. 2007. Citizen monitoring and restoration: volunteers and community involvement in wilderness stewardship. In: Watson, A.; Sproull, J.; Dean, L., comps. Science and stewardship to protect and sustain wilderness values: eighth world wilderness congress symposium. Proceedings RMRS-P-49. Fort Collins, CO: U.S. Department of Agriculture, Forest Service, Rocky Mountain Research Station: 101–106.